Middle Eastern CUISINE

Enslow PUBLISHING

COOKING WITH CULTURE

BY ANNA COLLINS

Please visit our website, www.enslow.com. For a free color catalog of all our high-quality books, call toll free 1-800-398-2504 or fax 1-877-980-4454.

Library of Congress Cataloging-in-Publication Data
Names: Collins, Anna, author.
Title: Middle Eastern cuisine / Anna Collins.
Description: Buffalo, New York : Enslow Publishing, [2025] | Series: Cooking with culture | Includes bibliographical references and index.
Identifiers: LCCN 2024002925 | ISBN 9781978540484 (library binding) | ISBN 9781978540477 (paperback) | ISBN 9781978540491 (ebook)
Subjects: LCSH: Cooking, Middle Eastern–Juvenile literature. | Food–Middle East–History–Juvenile literature. | LCGFT: Cookbooks.
Classification: LCC TX725.M628 C65 2025 | DDC 641.5956–dc23/eng/20240212
LC record available at https://lccn.loc.gov/2024002925

Published in 2025 by
Enslow Publishing
2544 Clinton Street
Buffalo, NY 14224

Portions of this work were originally authored by Roman Ayter and published as *Foods of the Middle East.* All new material in this edition authored by Anna Collins.

Designer: Leslie Taylor
Editor: Caitie McAneney

Photo credits: Cover (photo) Yulia Furman/Shutterstock.com; Series Art (background icon pattern) porcelaniq/Shutterstock.com; Series Art (series logo) lukeruk/Shutterstock.com; p. 5 Ivanna Pavliuk/Shutterstock.com; p. 7 SLSK Photography/Shutterstock.com; p. 9 diplomedia/Shutterstock.com; p. 11 (spices) Matej Kastelic/Shutterstock.com, (challah) OlgaBombologna/Shutterstock.com; p. 13 (meze) Akif_Cakmak_imgatemedia/Shutterstock.com, (dolmas) Aleksey Khoruzhenko/Shutterstock.com; p. 15 Rimma Bondarenko/Shutterstock.com; p. 17 Hashem Issam Alshanableh/Shutterstock.com; p. 19 Sea Wave/Shutterstock.com; p. 21 MShev/Shutterstock.com.

Printed in the United States of America

CPSIA compliance information: Batch #CSENS25: For further information contact Enslow Publishing at 1-800-398-2504.

Contents

Words in the glossary appear in **bold** type the first time they are used in the text.

Explore the Middle East

The area of Southwest Asia and North Africa is called the Middle East. The countries that make up this area are Bahrain, Egypt, Iran, Iraq, Israel, Jordan, Kuwait, Lebanon, Oman, Qatar, Saudi Arabia, Syria, Turkey, the United Arab Emirates, and Yemen. Other countries that are sometimes considered Middle Eastern are Afghanistan, Algeria, Cyprus, Libya, Morocco, Pakistan, Sudan, and Tunisia.

Hummus is a Middle Eastern dish that many people are familiar with.

The Middle East is home to many **cultures**! Different peoples share parts of their cultures, including their foods.

FOOD FOR THOUGHT

ARABS MAKE UP MOST OF THE POPULATION OF THE MIDDLE EAST. THERE ARE OTHER **ETHNIC** GROUPS THAT LIVE THERE, TOO.

A Long History

Civilization began in the Middle East! More than 10,000 years ago, people began to farm there. The first system of writing was created there, too.

Early Arab tribes drank goat's milk and ate foods such as dates and nuts. Persians ate fruits, rice, and meat such as duck.

FOOD FOR THOUGHT

ZA'ATAR IS A MIX OF SPICES USED ON MEATS, VEGETABLES, RICE, AND BREADS IN MIDDLE EASTERN COOKING.

Dates have long been a popular food in the Middle East. They grow on date palm trees.

They adopted foods from other places as their own, such as yogurt from Russia and spices from India and China. Trade made their dishes even more **diverse**.

Farming in the Middle East

Farming began in the Middle East in an area called the Fertile Crescent. This area had rich farmland. While many places in the Middle East were hot and dry, rich soil was found near rivers such as the Tigris and the Euphrates rivers in Iraq.

The main crops of the Middle East are wheat, corn, rice, and **barley**. People also grow olives, dates, grapes, tomatoes, and apples. The country of Yemen grows coffee to use and sell.

Eggplant is a popular vegetable in the Middle East. This chickpea dish called *fatteh* has grilled eggplant on top.

FOOD FOR THOUGHT

TODAY, DAMS, **IRRIGATION**, AND MACHINES MAKE IT EASIER TO GROW CROPS IN MANY MORE PLACES.

Familiar Foods

Many Middle Eastern foods use familiar spices, such as cumin, cardamom, allspice, and coriander. Saffron is a yellow Middle Eastern spice that comes from flowers. It's the most expensive spice in the world. Other common **ingredients** include honey, sesame seeds, and chickpeas.

FOOD FOR THOUGHT

PITA IS A FLAT BREAD THAT CAN BE OPENED AND FILLED WITH FOOD. OTHER BREADS INCLUDE THE JEWISH BRAIDED BREAD *CHALLAH* AND AN ARABIC BARLEY BREAD CALLED *FATIR*.

Spices add flavor and color to Middle Eastern dishes.

With each meal, bread is always on the table. Rice probably first arrived from India. Now it's eaten every day in countries such as Iran, Saudi Arabia, and Iraq.

One Meal, Many Foods

Meze is a great way to enjoy many different foods at once. Meze is a group of small dishes eaten at the same meal. It's popular in some Middle Eastern countries such as Turkey and Egypt. In some Arabic countries, the meze meal is called *muqabilat*.

FOOD FOR THOUGHT

DURING THE HOLY MONTH OF RAMADAN, MUSLIMS EAT A SPECIAL MEAL CALLED *IFTAR* AFTER SUNSET. MEZES ARE A BIG PART OF IFTAR.

meze

Dolmas are grape leaves stuffed with meat and rice. They're a popular meze dish.

Olives and pickles are often part of the selection. Nuts may also be served, as well as vegetables. Baba ghanoush is a creamy dip made of eggplant and sesame seeds. Another popular dip for meze is hummus.

Making Meat

Religion is often important to people in the Middle East. This sometimes affects what they eat, especially when it comes to meat. People who practice the Jewish and Muslim religions don't eat pork. In Arabic, the word *halal* means "permitted." Muslims eat halal meat and other foods.

FOOD FOR THOUGHT

LAMB IS A POPULAR MEAT IN MANY MIDDLE EASTERN COUNTRIES. LAMB STEW IS A POPULAR DISH WITH A LONG HISTORY.

Shish kebab is a dish made up of cubes of meat and vegetables roasted on a metal rod.

Meat is often spiced. Spiced meat is called *kofta* in Turkey and *kefta* in Arabic countries. People who live near the Persian Gulf—such as those in Bahrain and Kuwait—enjoy fish.

Pass the Pita!

Pita bread is eaten with many meals in the Middle East. It can be used as a side dish. It can be used with dips. It also holds food, such as falafel. Falafel is stuffed into pita and served with yogurt or tahini, a sauce made from sesame seeds.

Shawarma is another Middle Eastern "sandwich." Thin slices of meat are wrapped in pita, spread with hummus or tahini, and topped with vegetables.

FOOD FOR THOUGHT

FALAFEL IS A BALL OF MASHED CHICKPEAS THAT HAS BEEN SPICED AND FRIED IN OIL. IT'S ESPECIALLY POPULAR IN ISRAEL, SYRIA, QATAR, AND EGYPT.

Super Salads

Salads in the Middle East often involve small grains. *Tabbouleh*, the national dish of Lebanon, is a salad made of tomato, mint, and **bulgur**. It's scooped up with lettuce leaves. *Fattoush* is a salad of bread and vegetables. It's also especially popular in Lebanon.

Couscous is a tiny pasta that is used like rice. Lebanese couscous is larger than Israeli couscous. All kinds of ingredients may be added, such as carrots and raisins. Each cook may use their own ingredients and flavors.

Lebanese Tabbouleh

Ingredients

1/4 cup fine bulgur wheat
4 tablespoons olive oil
juice of 2 lemons
1/8 teaspoon black pepper
1/2 teaspoon salt
1 teaspoon crushed dried mint
2 cups curly parsley (finely chopped)
1 large tomato (diced)
5 scallions (finely sliced)
1/4 cup fresh mint (finely chopped)

Equipment

bowl
whisk

Steps

1. Using cold water, rinse the bulgur wheat. Cover it in a bowl with cold water.
2. Soak the bulgur for 15 minutes.
3. Pour the water out, leaving just the bulgur in the bowl.
4. In another small bowl, combine the lemon juice, salt, pepper, olive oil, and dried mint. This is your vinaigrette, or dressing.
5. In serving bowl, mix the bulgur with fresh mint, parsley, tomato, and scallion.
6. Pour the vinaigrette over the bulgur. Stir.

Delicious Desserts

Like many Middle Eastern dishes, desserts often include dates and nuts. Sugar, honey, and dates are often used to sweeten foods. Sweet treats include *qatayef*, which are also called "Arabic pancakes." They're filled with sweet cheese and nuts. A sweet, thick paste called *halwa* has flavors of sugar, honey, and spices.

Phyllo **pastry** is light and flaky. It's popular in Turkey and is used for desserts such as baklava. **Recipes** differ from country to country and cook to cook!

FOOD FOR THOUGHT

MANY COUNTRIES AROUND THE WORLD HAVE THEIR OWN VERSION OF RICE PUDDING. SPICES SUCH AS CARDAMOM, CINNAMON, AND NUTMEG ARE USED IN RICE PUDDING IN THE MIDDLE EAST.

Glossary

barley: A kind of grain.

bulgur: Dried wheat.

civilization: People living in an organized way.

culture: The beliefs and ways of life of a group of people.

diverse: Different or varied.

ethnic: Relating to large groups of people who have the same origin, religion, customs, and more.

ingredient: A part of a mixture.

irrigation: The watering of a dry area by man-made means in order to grow plants.

pastry: A mix of flour, water, and fat used for desserts such as pies.

recipe: An explanation of how to make a food.

religion: A belief in and way of honoring a god or gods.

For More Information

Books

Coleman, Miriam. *The Geography of Southwest Asia and North Africa*. New York, NY: PowerKids Press, 2021.

London, Martha. *The Middle East*. Lake Elmo, MN: Focus Readers, 2021.

Website

Middle East Geography
www.ducksters.com/geography/middleeast.php
Learn more about the geography of the Middle East!

Iraq
kids.nationalgeographic.com/geography/countries/article/iraq
Learn more about Iraq, the place where ancient civilizations started.

Publisher's note to educators and parents: Our editors have carefully reviewed these websites to ensure that they are suitable for students. Many websites change frequently, however, and we cannot guarantee that a site's future contents will continue to meet our high standards of quality and educational value. Be advised that students should be closely supervised whenever they access the internet.

Index